"The Chri
rooted in c
onstrates t
in history. There is a powerful reminder that Jesus is truly risen,
and this changes everything about our lives today."

Thomas R. Schreiner, James Buchanan Harrison
Professor of New Testament Interpretation,
The Southern Baptist Theological Seminary

"Well written, fast-paced, and filled with popular stories and
illustrations, this book takes up the challenging question of
whether Jesus's resurrection is a historical event. Follow Timothy
Paul Jones as he treks through nagging doubts and uncertainty,
one reasonable step at a time. If you are learning why the resurrection is true, this is the sort of book you want to read."

Gary R. Habermas, Distinguished Research Professor,
Liberty University School of Divinity

"Timothy Paul Jones utilizes an interdisciplinary approach to
provide a lucid, accessible, concise, and compelling case for the
historical fact of the bodily resurrection of Jesus Christ. This
book will serve as a conversation starter to help churches point
people to Jesus Christ as the exalted and risen Lord!"

Jarvis J. Williams, Professor of New Testament
Interpretation, The Southern Baptist
Theological Seminary

"With up-to-date scholarship and engaging prose, Timothy Paul Jones provides a compact text we can share with our university and seminary students to show them how to defend the resurrection in a winsome way. Highly recommended."

Mark Allen, Professor of Biblical and Theological Studies, Liberty University

"Jones blends the heart of a pastor with the precision of a scholar to tackle one of the most vital questions of our faith. He offers a relatable and compelling perspective, bringing to the church and skeptics alike a clear and convincing case for the resurrection."

Jamaal Williams, Pastor, Sojourn Midtown, Louisville, Kentucky

"Christianity rises or falls on a single historical claim: the resurrection of Jesus. This short, powerful book makes the case for the pivotal moment in human history. If you're curious about the unparalleled nature of Jesus, start your journey here."

J. Warner Wallace, *Dateline*-featured cold-case detective; Senior Fellow, the Colson Center for Christian Worldview

"The Christian faith is rooted in the historical resurrection of Jesus from the dead. Jones has written an accessible case for the resurrection of Jesus that is easy to read while carrying the weight of rigorous scholarship. This resource will prove valuable to both the skeptic and the believer wrestling with doubt."

Dayton Hartman, Lead Pastor, Redeemer Church, Rocky Mount, North Carolina

Did the Resurrection Really Happen?

TGC Hard Questions

Jared Kennedy, Series Editor

Did the Resurrection Really Happen?

Timothy Paul Jones

WHEATON, ILLINOIS

Did the Resurrection Really Happen?

© 2025 by Timothy Paul Jones

Published by Crossway
    1300 Crescent Street
    Wheaton, Illinois 60187

This book is published in association with Nappaland Literary Agency, an independent firm dedicated to publishing works that are: Authentic. Relevant. Eternal. Visit us on the web at: http://www.NappalandLiterary.com.

Cover design: Ben Stafford

Cover images: Unsplash

First printing 2025

Printed in the United States of America

Trade paperback ISBN: 978-1-4335-9855-5
ePub ISBN: 978-1-4335-9857-9
PDF ISBN: 978-1-4335-9856-2

Library of Congress Cataloging-in-Publication Data

Names: Jones, Timothy P. (Timothy Paul), author.
Title: Did the resurrection really happen? / Timothy Paul Jones.
Description: Wheaton, Illinois : Crossway, 2025. | Series: TGC hard questions | Includes bibliographical references and index.
Identifiers: LCCN 2024017391 (print) | LCCN 2024017392 (ebook) | ISBN 9781433598555 (trade paperback) | ISBN 9781433598562 (pdf) | ISBN 9781433598579 (epub)
Subjects: LCSH: Resurrection—Biblical teaching. | Jesus Christ—Resurrection.
Classification: LCC BS2655.R35 J66 2025 (print) | LCC BS2655.R35 (ebook) | DDC 236/.8—dc23/eng/20240917
LC record available at https://lccn.loc.gov/2024017391
LC ebook record available at https://lccn.loc.gov/2024017392

Crossway is a publishing ministry of Good News Publishers.

BP		34	33	32	31	30	29	28	27	26	25
15	14	13	12	11	10	9	8	7	6	5	4	3	2	1

Contents

A JEWISH NOBLE STARES UP the slope that terminates at the walls of Jerusalem. An arrow's shot from the walls, rugged knolls and hillocks flatten into a plain where twisted tree trunks are jammed into the earth. These trees are barren, with wooden beams affixed to them at a myriad of angles.

Dangling from the crossbeams are the flayed bodies of human beings.

The soldiers wandering among the crosses have vowed before the gods that they will enforce the will of Caesar no matter the cost. The men twisted in agony on the beams have been accused of insurrection against Caesar's will. As night falls and bodies fail, packs of wild dogs will arrive on the plain and plant their forelegs against the crosses, teeth bared and straining to rip away mangled muscles and exposed organs. Once the collapsing lungs of the crucified have squelched their last guttural breaths, vultures will descend on the carcasses, gorging themselves on congealing strips of skin.[1] Such is the fate of those sentenced to die on crosses.

The year is AD 70. The Roman legions are crushing a rebellion that began four years earlier. Faced with the imminent fall of their city, thousands of Jews have attempted escape, only to be captured and tortured on these barren trees. Today, as many as five hundred Jews will be nailed to the timbers outside the city. Hundreds will face the same fate tomorrow, and again the next day, and again and again until there are no trees left for miles around Jerusalem.

The name of the Jewish noble surveying the scene outside the city is Josephus. He is a Pharisee trying to convince his fellow Jews to give up their insurrection. Years later, Josephus will describe the abuse inflicted by the Romans on the captives: "Soldiers, out of the rage and spite they held . . . nailed them to the crosses in a variety of positions to ridicule them. Their number was so great that there . . . were not enough crosses for the bodies."[2]

This was far from the first or last time Roman soldiers crucified mass numbers of suspected insurrectionists. Over the span of centuries, the Romans repeated this practice with tens of thousands of rebels and slaves, spiking them to wooden beams in grotesque positions and leaving them to die. Suspended naked before the world, the cadavers of the crucified screamed a silent warning, declaring the inevitable demise of anyone who dared to defy the power of Rome. For dissidents and enslaved persons in particular, crucifixion loomed as a constant threat. Of the many thousands of victims who lived and died on the margins of the Roman social order, only the minutest fraction of names were recorded. Fewer still can be recalled today.

And yet, two thousand years after his death, the name of one crucified man is cherished around the globe.

This man was lynched on the outskirts of Jerusalem around AD 30, a generation before the city's destruction in AD 70. From the perspective of the rulers in Rome, his execution was insignificant and routine. Following a bit of unrest in the streets during a volatile Jewish festival, three suspects were stapled to crosses on a hill outside the city. The warning worked, at least from the Roman perspective. After this reminder not to provoke Rome's power, the Passover proceeded peaceably, with no riots or revolts reported.

But a revolution happened nonetheless.

According to a tiny band of faithful Jews, the cross did not mark the end for one of those three men. The message of his miraculous return to life would eventually engulf the very empire that had sentenced him to die. Today, this singular crucified man is not merely remembered. He is revered by billions as divine.

What Is So Different about Jesus?

But why should anyone think that out of all the thousands crucified by the Romans, this one victim of the cross returned to life, never to die again? It doesn't take many trips to the graveyard before you realize resurrection is far from the most common outcome for a corpse. Why suggest that this man's corpse didn't decay into dust like everyone else's?

What's so different about Jesus of Nazareth?

The entirety of Christianity stands or falls on the question of whether Jesus really returned from the dead. The apostle Paul stated as much in one of his letters: "If Christ has not been raised, your faith is futile and you are still in your sins" (1 Cor. 15:17). Either there was an empty tomb, or Christians have an empty faith. That's because if the life of Jesus ended when they laid him in the grave, there's no meaningful difference between him and all the other would-be messiahs executed by the Romans. "It is no great thing to believe that Christ died," an influential North African pastor named Augustine of Hippo told his people in the fifth century. "This is what matters to us, that we believe that he rose from the dead."[3] If Jesus is alive, heaven has made an appearance on earth, and that changes everything.

I don't know what you think about the resurrection of Jesus. Maybe you've never thought much about it. If that's the case, I hope this book challenges you to consider the immensity of the claim that Jesus is alive. Perhaps you've thought a lot about the resurrection, and the very notion that someone returned from the dead two thousand years ago seems absurd to you. If so, I'm glad we're on this journey together, because you're right to recognize that no one should make or take such a claim lightly.

Truth be told, I haven't always realized how outrageous it is to suggest that someone exited a stone-sealed cave on the third day after he was laid to rest. I lived nearly two decades before considering how preposterous such a claim might sound. When I was seventeen, all that began to change. That's when my credulous acceptance of Christian faith collapsed at a library desk in a college town in northeast Kansas.

That's also where the resurrection of Jesus began to matter to me like never before.

How the Resurrection Stopped Being a Problem and Started Being a Solution

I graduated from high school in the gap between glam metal and grunge, in the year that Germany was reunified and Alec Baldwin went on his hunt for Red October. In the churches my family attended during my later childhood and high school years, the King James Version of the Bible was the only Bible accepted, neither the Bible nor the pastor could ever be questioned, all contemporary music and entertainment was to be avoided, and every barrier between us and the rest of the world had to be built high.

Then I went to college.

It was a Christian college, and the professors believed the Bible. But none of them believed the Bible like I'd been taught to believe it. My studies quickly plunged me into a dark corridor of doubt. One of the discoveries that troubled me most came from a book I ran across while writing a paper for a New Testament class. According to this book, the resurrection of a divine being wasn't a unique notion in the ancient world. People had believed in the death and resurrection of gods like Attis and Horus and Osiris centuries before Jesus, and early Christians may have borrowed the resurrection from these myths.[4] So the story of the resurrection was not surprising from the perspective of ancient people—or so the author suggested.

Around this time, I was offered a job at the college library. Each evening, it was my responsibility to shelve the books that had been returned that day. I remember noticing the title of one particular collection of essays one night as I slid the volume into its spot on the shelf. It was *Why I Am Not a Christian*, and the author was a philosopher named Bertrand Russell. The bluntness of the title appealed to my growing sense of frustration toward the only form of Christianity I knew, and I began reading the book on the way back to my desk.

In the titular essay, Russell declared with disarming confidence that "historically it is quite doubtful whether Christ ever existed at all, and if he did we do not know anything about him."[5] Years later, I recognize that Russell's words ignore a vast breadth of historical evidence. No reputable historian today doubts that Jesus existed or that the Romans crucified him.[6] But I didn't know that then. In that moment, Russell's words unleashed yet another torrent of doubt within me. The more I read, the more it seemed like Jesus—the deity I had once trusted without question—might be as mythical as the gods of Egypt and Greece and Rome. The resurrection of Jesus, in particular, began to seem like a problem. If the claims of resurrections in other religions are mythical, why should I think the same claims are historical when they're applied to Jesus?

Is there really anything different about Jesus?

For the first time in my life, I began to sense the strangeness of supposing a once-deceased man left his tomb alive and well nearly two thousand years ago. Yet I also recognized that without the resurrection of Jesus, there is no Christian faith worth believing. Increasingly, my primary concern turned toward the question of how I would tell the people who knew me best that I had left my faith behind.

It was an Irishman whose name I previously knew only from novels who first opened my mind to a new set of possibilities. Some of C. S. Lewis's fictional works had been banned in one of the Christian schools I attended as a teenager (to this day, I'm still not sure why). As a result, I was intrigued when I was shelving books and discovered this professor of literature had produced dozens of books and essays defending the logical and historical coherence of the Christian faith.

The text from Lewis that most captivated me was *Surprised by Joy*, a meandering spiritual autobiography that traced the professor's journey from atheism to theism and finally to Christianity. What I realized as I read *Surprised by Joy* was that losing my religion wasn't the only possible response to the doubts I was experiencing. What's more, certain questions that seemed new and shocking to me—the possibility that there were parallels between the Gospels and pagan myths, for example—weren't really new at all.

This became more apparent to me when I ran across one of Lewis's essays entitled "Myth Became Fact." When considering parallels between ancient myths and the stories of Jesus, Lewis didn't deny the existence of at least a few similarities. Instead, he opened the door to new ways of seeing the parallels, and he showed how the similarities were not nearly as similar as some scholars seemed to suggest.

The old myth of the Dying God, without ceasing to be myth, comes down from the heaven of legend and imagination to the earth of history. It happens—at a particular date, in a particular place, followed by definable historical consequences. We pass from a Balder or an Osiris, dying nobody knows when or where, to a historical Person crucified . . . under Pontius Pilate.[7]

Soon, I was reading the writings of Lewis alongside the skeptical texts that had sustained and multiplied so many of my doubts. Along the way, I found more books that included evidence for the reliability of the Gospels and the resurrection of Jesus. *The New Testament Documents: Are They Reliable?* by F. F. Bruce affected me deeply, and so did Josh McDowell's *More Than a Carpenter*. Looking back, I realize that some of these texts were better grounded in historical evidence than others, but all of them opened new gateways in my mind.

At some point in all this reading, something started to shift. It seemed like there may be something different about Jesus after all. In the months that followed, the resurrection of Jesus increasingly appeared less like a problem and more like a possible solution. I was still struggling to believe, and I still found myself abandoning many false claims I'd heard in the churches of my childhood. Yet, the more I held on and dug into the evidence, the harder it became for me to maintain my skepticism about the resurrection.

When I compared the New Testament with other ancient texts, I began to see that, whether or not the Gospel authors were telling the truth, they clearly intended their writings to describe real events in human history. What's more, at least some of their testimony seemed traceable to eyewitnesses. Perhaps most significantly, explaining away the martyrdoms of those who knew Jesus was a lot more difficult than I had previously thought. Why would some of these witnesses maintain their testimonies all the way to death if they had not experienced something extraordinary, perhaps even supernatural?

Little by little, the evidences eroded my skepticism. A few months later—not all at once but subtly and slowly, like a morning walk that begins in starlight but ends in sunlight and you cannot recall exactly when the dark turned to dawn—a glimmer of confidence pierced the surface of my consciousness again. I had left behind the cultural trappings of the churches of my childhood, but I believed in the crucified and risen Jesus more than ever before. The repercussions of this newfound confidence redirected my entire life.

How Can We Know Whether the Resurrection Happened in History?

Today, more than three decades after I first read *Why I Am Not a Christian*, I eagerly embrace every essential claim that seemed so unbelievable during those months of doubt. I believe in a Jewish Messiah who drew his first breaths between a virgin's knees. I believe in a wandering teacher who was crucified but who returned from the dead on the third day. I believe this divine Messiah is also the second person of the triune God. I am convinced that the same three-personed God who crafted the cosmos in the beginning will someday recreate the world and flood every crest and crevasse of the universe with justice. I do not accept any of these tenets blindly. Yet, the deeper I've delved into the claims of Christianity, the more I believe this faith remains the best explanation of reality, particularly when it comes to the question of the resurrection. When I examine historical texts and artifacts, I find good reasons to believe Jesus was unlike any other man crucified by the Romans, yet also unlike any god described in ancient myths. His resurrection is only implausible if we presuppose a world where miracles are impossible.

I'm convinced there really is something different about Jesus.

When it comes to what's different about him, the resurrection stands as the cornerstone. The bodies of other perceived threats to the peace of Rome expired on their crosses, and their bodies decomposed. The myths of dying-and-rising gods describe deities who never lived at all. Jesus left a mark in history that suggests he lived and died but didn't stay dead. Historically speaking, that's what's so different about Jesus.

But how can anyone be confident that the resurrection really happened?

In a book as brief as this one, I can't dispel every doubt or provide every piece of evidence for the resurrection. My hopes are far more modest. I simply want you to recognize that the first followers of Jesus didn't claim their leader rose from the dead because of gullible ignorance or blind faith. They knew dead people stay dead. Especially after they began to be persecuted, they had nothing to gain by persisting in their claim that Jesus had returned to life. Yet some of these women and men had encountered an event so momentous they were ready to die rather than deny they saw a once-dead man alive. These initial eye-witnesses declared what they experienced, and in some cases they died for what they declared. At least a few of their firsthand testimonies eventually found their way into the New Testament.

Even if you think the resurrection of Jesus and the existence of a "Flying Spaghetti Monster" are equally preposterous, the testimonies of the first generation of witnesses should not be dismissed lightly. Something upended the lives of these men and women and made them willing to die for what they believed they had seen. After decades of studying the historical aftermath of these events, I still believe the resurrection makes the best sense of the evidence.

What Faith Is—and Isn't

For at least a few of you, it may sound strange that I am mentioning evidence in the same context as faith. Maybe you have understood the word *faith* the way biologist Richard Dawkins defines the term: "Faith is a state of mind that leads people to believe something—it doesn't matter what—in the total absence of supporting evidence." Dawkins later declares, "People believe in the resurrection not because of good evidence (there isn't any) but because, if the resurrection is not true, Christianity becomes null and void."[8] Dawkins is right to recognize that without the resurrection, Christianity is meaningless. Where Dawkins swerves into the wrong lane is in his claim that faith is the enemy of evidence.

If that is what you think when you hear the word *faith*, it may be helpful for you to know that faith, at least as it was understood among the earliest Christians, has never stood in opposition to evidence. Faith is a disposition of confidence that includes evidence. "They are very much in error," declared Augustine, "who think that we believe in Christ without any proofs of Christ."[9] Faith may entail more than mere acceptance of evidence, but it certainly includes no less. Far from eschewing evidence, faith seeks evidence. At its best, faith is even open to reconfiguration in response to better evidence.

Once we understand that faith and evidence aren't enemies, we begin to see that everyone lives by faith. All of us trust in presuppositions and possibilities we cannot prove beyond every possible doubt, and none of us believes all we believe solely on the basis of evidence. "When we confront the claim of the resurrection," pastor Tim Keller once pointed out, "we address it not only with logic but with a lifetime of hopes and fears and preexisting faith commitments."[10] This reality is not limited to Christians. Many agnostics and atheists also acknowledge the fact that faith is not limited to religious people. Bart Ehrman, speaking as an agnostic biblical scholar, admits: "Everybody has faith in something. My agnosticism is a kind of faith."[11] Rhett McLaughlin of the duo Rhett and Link had this to say when he reflected on his rejection of Christianity:

> There's a tendency for people like me, who've not only deconstructed but deconverted, to just . . . believe that you no longer have faith. . . . But the thing that I'm realizing is that . . . I'm still human, and I believe that faith is a feature of humanity. . . . I wholeheartedly believe that the things that I'm going to tell you are not things that I can prove.[12]

Every human being lives by faith. The question is not whether we have faith. The question is how closely our faith fits with reality.

If you are skeptical of Christian claims about the resurrection, here is all I am asking of you as you read this book: Are you open-minded enough to consider the possibility that there is a power that can reverse death? If you are, would you at least consider the evidences for the resurrection and see where the evidence leads?

A Fact to Which We Can Call Witnesses

After years of wrestling with the evidence, I remain convinced there is something different about Jesus. Unlike any other human being in all of human history, he died and returned to life, never to die again.

When you reach the end of this book, you may agree with me that a crucified man was once raised from the dead, or you might not. Either way, my hope is that you will at least recognize these claims are not made without evidence. "This is," British journalist G. K. Chesterton once pointed out, "the sort of truth that is hard to explain because it is a fact; but it is a fact to which we can call witnesses."[13]

Now it is time to call some witnesses.

How Did the Stories of the Resurrection Start?

Imagine a scene with me.

A middle-aged grandmother is working on the front porch of her Kentucky farmhouse. The woman hears an odd pattering beside the house. She can't see the side yard from her perch on the front porch, so she sends her grandson to take a look. When the boy returns, he claims it is snowing. The clear blue sky on this late winter's day suggests otherwise.

The grandmother bustles down the steps and rounds the house. Suddenly, she is shocked by a sight she never imagined.

Fragments of raw meat are falling from the sky.

Some scraps are the size of a small saucer, most are more like snowflakes, but all of them are unexpected. The meatfall lasts less than an hour and leaves about a half-bushel of meat scattered in the side yard. Before the day is over, reports of the carnal downpour pass from house to house, and neighbors trickle down the lane to glimpse the rarity with their own eyes. The story quickly reaches beyond the borders of Kentucky. A reporter from the *New York Herald* shows up to investigate, and he leaves convinced the woman is telling the truth.

But, of course, everyone knows meat cannot just fall from the sky. Except, at least once, it did.

On March 3, 1876, a two-hour drive east of my house, a grandmother named Mrs. Crouch reported to her neighbors that she witnessed bits of meat spilling from a clear sky. Some of the fragments are preserved today in the science department of a university in Lexington, Kentucky.[14] Although the precise origin of the carnal rain remains uncertain, researchers then and now remain confident the event actually happened.

But how could anyone believe such a story?

Stories begin with experiences, expectations, imagination, or sometimes all of the above. The story of the Kentucky meat shower is no exception. This story began with multiple witnesses who never imagined anything like this could happen, yet these same witnesses testified that it did happen and they experienced it. Part of the reason this story is so believable is that attributing the story to people's imaginations cannot adequately explain the testimonies of those who were there. Reports from when and where the alleged event took place don't guarantee that the event happened, but such testimonies do make the claims far more credible.[15]

Which brings me back to the claim that Jesus rose from the dead.

Regardless of what you think about whether Jesus is dead or alive, the stories about him did not burst fully formed from the leather-bound pages of your Bible like Athena erupting from the forehead of Zeus. The resurrection story started somewhere.

But where and how could such a story begin?

I have already pointed out that the resurrection is an event to which we can call witnesses. The first witnesses I will call are multiple women and men who claimed they saw Jesus alive after he had died. But, on the way to calling these witnesses, I want to take seriously one alternative possibility: *What if people in the ancient Roman Empire were already expecting something like the resurrection of a god or messiah?*

Unlike a meat shower in the nineteenth century, maybe the resurrection was an event first-century people were already looking for. If so, maybe the story did not start with any actual experience. Perhaps a band of disappointed disciples were already expecting a resurrection, so they manufactured this story to match their own anticipations.

This potential problem has been raised many times before, and it is one that Christians should take seriously. So, before bringing the earliest testimonies about the resurrection to the witness stand, we will first take a quick look at what first-century people may have expected to happen after Jesus died.

A Story Taken from Tales of Heroes and Gods?

Could it be that Christians based the story of Jesus on earlier tales of pagan heroes or dying-and-rising gods? This is one of the oldest arguments against the resurrection of Jesus. A philosopher named Celsus made this case in the second century, comparing the resurrection of Jesus to the mysterious disappearance and return of a well-known poet.[16] According to a more recent writer, the stories of Jesus are so similar to the stories of the Egyptian god Horus that early Christians must have ripped off the resurrection from the Egyptians.[17] Might the early church have constructed a tale of resurrection from stories like these?

When I struggled with my faith throughout my first year of college, this question haunted me more deeply than almost any other dilemma. Today, the problem of pagan parallels does not concern me at all. Here is why:

First, even if parallels do exist between the myths of the gods and the resurrection of Jesus, that does not require us to reduce the resurrection to fiction. Such parallels might be—as Lewis observed decades ago—expressions of innate human longings for atonement and new life.[18]

Second, the parallels themselves are problematic. In fact, when ancient texts and artifacts are analyzed, the parallels are not as parallel as the skeptics claim. Despite widespread claims that gods like Horus were crucified and resurrected, no such story can be located in any pre-Christian depiction or descriptions. For example, a monument illustrating the story of Horus does not depict him as crucified or resurrected, as some skeptics suggest. Instead, Horus was portrayed by the Egyptians to have been stung by a poisonous creature and revived by his mother and a moon god—a fate very different from crucifixion followed by resurrection.[19] A close examination of the stories of other gods reveals similar gaps.

In the handful of narratives that do describe the spiritual death and return of a deity, the stories typically function as metaphors for the yearly shift from winter to spring that turns fallow fields fertile again. But the story that early Christians told was never that Jesus was raised in a spiritual or metaphorical sense. If such a tale had been told about Jesus in the first century, the story would have been unremarkable, unobjectionable, and quickly forgotten.

The earliest Christian writings told a far more radical story. They depicted Jesus as human and divine, born in Bethlehem during the reign of Caesar Augustus (Luke 2:1–7) and into a family that eventually included siblings who were well-known in the churches (Rom. 1:3; 9:5; 1 Cor. 9:5; 15:5). According to the first generation of Christians, the same flesh of Jesus that entered the world through Mary's womb died and rose again in the course of ordinary human history (Rom. 6:10; Gal. 1:1; 4:4; 1 Pet. 3:18). The result of this resurrection was a transformed body that could consume a fish fillet, cook breakfast, and be grasped by the trembling fingers of those who loved him (Luke 24:42–43; John 20:17; 21:9). The resurrection of Jesus was nothing like the nebulous ghost of Obi-Wan Kenobi appearing to Luke Skywalker in *The Empire Strikes Back*. It was more like Gandalf in *The Lord of the Rings* returning in the flesh after he died and "strayed out of thought and time" before being sent back—except that unlike J. R. R. Tolkien, the early Christians did not intend their accounts to be read as fiction.[20]

Unlike the metaphorical returns of dying-and-rising gods, the resurrection described by Christians was "a one-time, historical event that took place at one specific point in the earth's topography," "unrelated to seasonal changes."[21] It seems inconceivable that early Christians could have derived this sort of resurrection from seasonal cycles of dying-and-rising gods.

If the dying-and-rising gods can't explain the resurrection, what about the heroic exploits found in ancient novels and plays, with their heroes and heroines who miraculously cheated death? Could the resurrection of Jesus have been borrowed from stories like these? It is true that protagonists in ancient tales did frequently find ways to escape the domains of the dead. In a story by the playwright Euripides, for example, Hercules dueled death and restored a woman to life.[22] Yet those who saw such stories enacted on stages never supposed a physical resurrection might actually take place.[23] Plato and several other ancient writers did suppose that stars and souls were made from the same stuff—a point of view that made a surprising reappearance in the song "I'm a Star" in Disney's animated fantasy Wish. Because of the widespread belief in a common origin of souls and stars, the ascent of virtuous souls to the stars was a common theme. Yet astral ascent is very different from bodily resurrection.[24]

Lots of people in the first century believed their spirits could outlast their epitaphs and even ascend to the heavens, but bodily resurrection was not an option ancient Romans seriously considered. In the minds of most, the body could provide pleasures and attain glory while on the earth. Yet, after ridding oneself of the body, no one would want it, or anything like it, back again.[25] The spirits of the dead might descend to Hades or ascend to the stars, but one thing spirits did not do was return to flesh and bone on the earth.

A Story Fabricated as a Fulfillment of Jewish Expectations?

If the ancient tales of heroes and gods can't explain the resurrection story, what about the expectations of the Jewish people? Jesus was Jewish, after all. If the Jews were already hoping for resurrection, might a Jewish community concoct the tale of Jesus's resurrection to deal with the crushing aftermath of his crucifixion? Could this explain the rise and spread of a belief in his bodily resurrection?

Not really.

In the first place, not all first-century Jews were looking for a future resurrection.[26] Even if we limit this explanation to Jews who were expecting a resurrection, it is still problematic. The resurrection that the followers of Jesus described was nothing like the resurrection Jewish sects were looking for.

Jews who anticipated resurrection were expecting God to raise all the righteous at the end of time. None of them anticipated the resurrection of an individual or group of individuals prior to the end of this age.[27]

Even if someone might have considered an individual resurrection before the end of time, no one envisioned the Messiah as the one who would be raised from the dead. Jesus was far from the only messianic figure to die at the hands of the Romans. In the very years when the stories of Jesus were spreading across the empire, Rome executed a number of would-be messiahs. They beheaded Theudas, hurled Simon bar Giora to his death from the Tarpeian Rock, and killed Simon bar Kokhba in battle. Yet no one expected any of these messianic figures to return from the dead. The reason no such claim circulated is that it was not what any of the Jews in this era anticipated.[28]

So, first-century cultural expectations are not sufficient to explain how the story of the resurrection of Jesus got started. At the time this story began to spread, worshipers of the Roman gods were not looking for bodily resurrection at all, and the Jews had reserved resurrection for the end of time. Then as now, people expected the dead to stay dead. The rationale for doubting the resurrection today might differ from the reasons people would have given in the first century, but the finality of death is not a modern discovery. First-century people knew death was a one-way street. Claiming a corpse returned to life was no less strange then than it is now.

A Story Traceable to the Time and Place the Events Occurred

So what else might explain the rise and spread of the story that Jesus rose from the dead?

One very plausible possibility is that the story began with some sort of powerful experience that affected the lives of multiple people. According to the earliest textual sources, the narrative of the resurrection emerged from the experiences of women and men who sincerely believed they saw Jesus alive in the days that followed his death.

Such testimonies do not guarantee their claims are true, of course. Eyewitness reports can be mistaken, and a claim might be true with or without firsthand testimony. At the same time, testimonies from when and where an alleged event took place do increase the credibility of the claims made.

With that thought in mind, it may help to look at the earliest testimonies about the resurrection of Jesus. Here is the question I want to consider: Can any of these reports be traced back to the time and place the alleged event happened?

I am convinced they can be.

The resurrection is an event to which we can call witnesses, and these witnesses include reports that are traceable to the people, places, and communities where sightings of a resurrected Jesus were first reported. The more closely I examine these texts, the more plausible it seems to me that the stories started with a series of experiences that the first witnesses could not fit into ordinary categories.

One of the most important summaries of the resurrection is a creed the apostle Paul incorporated into one of his letters. Long before "Creed" referred to a 1990s rock band or a twenty-first-century spinoff from the *Rocky* films, *creed* denoted a summation of beliefs that Christians share.

Believers in Jesus have repeated many creeds over the centuries, but one of the earliest is recorded in Paul's first letter to the church in Corinth. Even though Paul penned this summation, he was not the one who created it. Someone had passed the creed to Paul, and Paul had repeated the summary of events and witnesses when he visited the Corinthians three or so years before he wrote this letter.[29] Here's the outline of faith Paul recalled in his letter:

> . . . that Christ died for our sins in accordance with the Scriptures, that he was buried, that he was raised on the third day in accordance with the Scriptures, and that he appeared to Cephas, then to the twelve. Then he appeared to more than five hundred brothers at one time, most of whom are still alive, though some have fallen asleep. Then he appeared to James, then to all the apostles. (1 Cor. 15:3–7)

This summary includes every crucial truth Christians confess about the resurrection of Jesus. According to the creed, the body of Jesus was not abandoned in a pile of cadavers or left on a cross to be consumed by beasts and birds ("he was buried"). Jesus didn't ascend physically into the heavens from the cross; his resurrection was a bodily transformation that took place after his death and burial ("he was raised on the third day").[30] Perhaps most important, whatever happened to Jesus was not a private occurrence. Numerous people insisted they saw him after his death, and Christians in Paul's own day could still interview eyewitnesses who said they had seen Jesus alive.

But where and how did Paul receive this creed in the first place?

The outline Paul recorded in 1 Corinthians almost certainly came from Jerusalem, the very location where Jesus was crucified and where some of his followers later claimed they saw him alive. Not only that, but the creed can also be traced to a time when firsthand witnesses of the life and ministry of Jesus were still alive and leading the Jerusalem church.

So why can we be confident that this creed came from when and where the alleged events took place? The only individuals mentioned by name in the creed are Cephas and James. *Cephas* is the equivalent in the Aramaic language of *Peter*, and James was a brother of Jesus. These two men, both of whom knew Jesus personally, were "pillars" in the Jerusalem church in AD 30 (Gal. 2:6–9). The creed mentions their names without any modifiers or explanations, suggesting that the words took shape in a context where both were familiar faces. Taken together, everything we see in this summation of faith points to an origin in Jerusalem soon after the events took place.[31]

So when could Paul have heard this snippet of summarized testimony? Paul embraced Jesus as his Messiah within a couple of years of Jesus's execution at most.[32] Three years after this reorientation of his life, Paul headed to Jerusalem and spent fifteen days talking with Peter there (Gal. 1:18; see also Acts 9:26–30). Paul most likely received this outline of faith no later than those weeks he spent with Peter in Jerusalem, which means the creed reached Paul five years or less after Jesus's death.

Of course, it is very possible Paul had heard this summation before his visit to Jerusalem, but it certainly does not seem he would have received these words any later. The next time we encounter Paul after his stopover in Jerusalem, he is already being sent out to share the message of Jesus in Cyprus and Asia Minor (Acts 13:2–14:28). In every place he visited, Paul apparently delivered the same creedal content, and he wasn't significantly modifying what he received. Even though the Corinthians received this letter three or so years after Paul left their city, the apostle was confident the church would remember what he had told them earlier. If Paul had not been passing on the same outline of faith in every place, he could not have expected the Corinthians to recall what he had said when he was with them in person.

Stories from the Land Where Jesus Lived

And so, the content of the creed can be traced back to a time and a place where people had firsthand knowledge of Jesus—but it is not only the creed in 1 Corinthians 15:3–7 that originated when and where these witnesses were living. The resurrection stories in the Gospels can also be traced to individuals with firsthand knowledge of Jesus.

No one knows for certain where the New Testament Gospels were written, but it is possible to reconstruct certain aspects of where the stories originated. Here is what seems clear based on information inside and outside the Gospels: The stories that were eventually woven into the Gospels originated in locations where the alleged events happened. So why can we be confident when it comes to the regions where these stories originated? The Gospel narratives repeatedly describe very specific topographical trivia that could only have come from people with firsthand knowledge of the regions where the events took place.

The author of Mark's Gospel knew it was possible, for example, to proceed directly from the Sea of Galilee into the Galilean hill country—a detail that, while accurate, would have been virtually unknown outside that region (Mark 3:7, 13; see also Matt. 14:22–23; 15:29). John's Gospel records an even more obscure fact, correctly describing the path from Cana to Capernaum as downhill (John 2:12). All four Gospels repeatedly reference the fact that a journey to Jerusalem required going uphill (Matt. 20:17–18; Mark 10:32–33; Luke 2:42; 10:30–31; 18:31; 19:28; John 2:13; 5:1; 7:8–14; 11:55; 12:20). These are only a tiny sample from hundreds of examples that reveal intimate knowledge of the regional topography as well as typical names of people who resided in these locations.[33] No one could have known such minutiae without either trekking the terrain in person or writing down detailed testimonies recounted by witnesses who lived in these lands. No maps in this era showed elevations, inclines, or obscure links between locations, and no detailed geographic descriptions of Judea or Galilee survive in any first-century texts.

If second-century accounts of the authorship of the Gospels are correct, these details make sense. Early Christian sources describe the author of Mark's Gospel as the "follower and translator" of Peter who recorded Peter's retellings of the stories of Jesus after years of hearing them. The Gospels according to Matthew and Luke borrowed much of Mark's material, but Luke was also a companion of Paul who added information from "eyewitnesses and ministers of the word" to his Gospel (Luke 1:2), while Matthew's Gospel includes recollections from the apostle Matthew and perhaps other sources as well. Second-century Christian writings repeatedly mention that the Gospel of John originated with a firsthand follower of Jesus whose name was John.[34] If the New Testament Gospels do indeed preserve the words of Peter, John, and others who walked these regions, it is no wonder the texts get so many topographical details correct.

The New Testament Gospels may have been composed in Ephesus or Rome or any number of other cities, but those locations were not where the stories started. The testimonies that have been twined together in the Gospels originated among persons with firsthand knowledge of Judea and Galilee. What's more, their stories were retold so carefully that seemingly trivial details were safeguarded as the testimonies spread. Whatever happened to Jesus happened—in the words of Lewis—"at a particular date, in a particular place, followed by definable historical consequences," and early Christians preserved the details of these places as they repeated the stories.[35]

These details have profound implications for the question of whether or not the resurrection happened. All four New Testament Gospels agree that the body of Jesus was buried, that his body exited the tomb on the third day, and that witnesses saw him alive. If the other stories in the Gospels originated among people in the places where the alleged events occurred, the resurrection stories most likely did as well. Reports of the risen Jesus were not fabricated decades after his death among people who never knew him. The reports can be traced instead to firsthand experiences in and around the city where Jesus was crucified.

Which brings me back to those bits of meat that landed in northern Kentucky more than a century ago.

The Kentucky meat shower was a shocking event that did not fit anyone's existing categories. Yet people believed it, even when they could not explain it, due in part to the quality of the testimonies. The initial reports could be traced to witnesses in the place where the event occurred, among people who were not expecting anything like this to happen.

I am not suggesting a total correspondence between these two events, of course. The resurrection as it was described by the first followers of Jesus would require the existence of some higher reality, whereas the Kentucky meat shower does not appear to have been supernatural at all. Most researchers today have concluded the fragments of meat landed in Mrs. Crouch's yard because a flock of vultures vomited far above her farmhouse after being frightened by a bird of prey.[36] The mysterious meatfall was, however, a seemingly unprecedented event that remained unexplained for some time. Yet people believed the story based on the testimony of eyewitnesses and neighbors in the time and location that the alleged event took place.

Jack's Beanstalk and Jesus Christ

"Accounts of Jesus' resurrection and ascension are," atheist Richard Dawkins has declared, "about as well-documented as Jack and the Beanstalk."[37] Whether or not you think Jesus is alive, I hope it is clear to you by now that skepticism of this sort ignores a vast array of historical sources from the first and second centuries. Stories of the risen Jesus originated among witnesses of his life in locations where he lived and died. No testimony about Jack or his beanstalk can be traced back to witnesses who saw the stalk ascending skyward in the very place where Jack tossed his beans on the ground.

The resurrection story does not come without difficulties, but it also does not come without credible evidence. It is a story no one in the first century expected to be true. Yet a band of witnesses became convinced they saw Jesus alive in the flesh in the days that followed his death, and their reports can be traced to the places Jesus lived and died. The quality of these testimonies does not necessarily require that God raised Jesus from the dead, but such testimonies provide credible evidence that should not be lightly dismissed (see table 1).

Table 1. Origins of the resurrection story

What Is the Witness?	Where Did the Witness Originate?	When Did the Witness Originate?	What Is the Content of the Witness?
1 Cor. 15:3–7	References to "Cephas" (Peter), "James," and "the twelve" suggest the summary originated in the Jerusalem church.	The creed was passed on as oral history in the decade of the 30s and written in the 50s.	Jesus died and was raised on the third day and was seen by Cephas, the twelve, more than five hundred believers, James, and all the apostles.
Mark 16:1–8 (adapted in Matt. 28:1–4 and Luke 24:1–4)	Geographic details suggest the narratives originated with persons living in regions of Judea and Galilee.	The gospel was written in the second half of the first century AD, based on eyewitness testimony from Peter.	Jesus died and was raised on the third day; Mary Magdalene was one of the first witnesses at the empty tomb.
John 20:1–18	Geographic details suggest the narratives originated with persons living in regions of Judea and Galilee.	The gospel was written in the second half of the first century AD, based on eyewitness testimony from John.	Jesus died and was raised on the third day; Mary Magdalene was one of the first witnesses at the empty tomb.

Why Should Anyone Believe the Witnesses?

Before becoming a father, I never imagined how much of parenting consists of finding the right tactics to determine whether or not your children are telling the truth.

Suppose I step into the family room and see a hole in the drywall that wasn't there before. Despite clear evidence that something suspicious has taken place, every one of my children denies any knowledge of how a wall might have mysteriously developed an eight-inch indentation (true story).

Faced with such circumstances, I have sometimes separated my daughters into different rooms and asked each individual to tell me what happened. If two or more children who have not colluded with each other tell me the same story, it is worth considering the possibility that they are the ones telling the truth. That is especially true when one of my children admits particular details that do not place her in the best light. Imagine, for example, that one of my daughters admits she and her sister were listening to music and practicing gymnastics when they had been told to do their chores. Let us further imagine this child confesses that her accomplice in these misdemeanors misjudged a handstand and put her knee through the wall. Now, suppose that the accomplice who is about to be indicted for vandalizing the family room is also inexplicably limping (also a true story). Case closed.

The same principles that have helped me solve so many complicated parenting cases can also help in the practice of history. When multiple independent sources agree on the key contours of a story, it is worth considering that the narrative they share may be credible. That is especially true when this shared story includes details that do not place the storyteller in the best light.

So what does all of this have to do with whether or not the resurrection really happened?

When it comes to the story of Jesus's resurrection, multiple independent sources agree on the same general sequence of events. Every retelling of the resurrection mentions that Jesus died, that he was buried, that he was raised on the third day, and that he appeared to specific individuals and groups. All four New Testament Gospels, as well as a later independent retelling of the resurrection preserved in the manuscript Papyrus Cairo 10759, identify Mary Magdalene as the first witness at the empty tomb.[38] When it comes to when and how Jesus died, the eminent Roman historian Tacitus agrees with the Gospel writers that Jesus was crucified in Judea during the administration of Pontius Pilate.[39]

Taken together, these points represent a striking conflux of reports scattered throughout a series of separate sources (see table 2). Plus, there is one particular detail no one would have fabricated: Mary Magdalene as the initial witness.

If this story had been concocted by first-century followers of Jesus, no one would have positioned a woman at the empty tomb. In the contexts where Christianity first took root and grew, women were not regarded as trustworthy witnesses.[40] The presence of this inconvenient detail in the resurrection story suggests that early Christians were willing to preserve the truth about what happened even when it was awkward. Prioritizing a woman's testimony makes no sense unless Mary Magdalene actually was the first witness at the tomb.

Table 2. Agreement among the witnesses to the resurrection

	Jerusalem Creed	Mark	Matthew	Luke	John	Papyrus Cairo 10759
Jesus died.	"died" (1 Cor. 15:3)	"breathed his last" (15:33–41)	"yielded up his spirit" (27:45–56)	"breathed his last" (23:44–49)	"gave up his spirit" (19:28–37)	"was taken up" (5)
Jesus was buried.	"buried" (15:4a)	"laid him in a tomb" (15:42–47)	"laid it [his body] in his [Joseph's] own new tomb" (27:57–61)	"laid him in a tomb" (23:50–55)	"a new tomb.... They laid Jesus there." (19:38–42)	"brought him into his [Joseph's] own tomb" (6–7)
The empty tomb was witnessed first by Mary Magdalene.		"Mary Magdalene . . . went." (16:1–5)	"Mary Magdalene . . . went." (28:1–4)	"It was Mary Magdalene." (23:55–24:3, 10)	"Mary Magdalene came." (20:1–2)	"Mary Magdalene . . . took her friends." (12)

	Jerusalem Creed	Mark	Matthew	Luke	John	Papyrus Cairo 10759
Jesus was raised on the third day.	"raised on the third day" (15:4b)	"risen" (16:6) "in three days" (15:29)	"after three days . . . risen" (27:63; 28:5–8)	"risen . . . on the third day" (24:4–12)	"must rise" (20:3–10) "in three days" (2:19–20)	"three days . . . risen" (8, 13)
Jesus appeared to individuals.	"Cephas, . . . James" (15:5a, 7a)	"Peter" (16:7)	"my brothers" (28:9–10)	"two of them, . . . one of them, named Cleopas" (24:13–32)	"my brothers" (20:11–18)	"Simon Peter and Andrew . . . and Levi" (14, ms. incomplete)
Jesus appeared to gathered disciples.	"the twelve" (15:5b)	"his disciples" (16:7)	"the eleven disciples" (28:16–20)	"the eleven" (24:33–51)	"the disciples . . . the twelve" (20:19–29)	"the twelve disciples" (14, ms. incomplete)

Something Actually Rooted in History

The striking consistency of these reports, even when it comes to inconvenient details, is one reason why many skeptics agree that at least some parts of the story must have happened. The resurrection is a story to which we can call witnesses, and some of these witnesses are not even Christians. Bart Ehrman was an agnostic who recently has begun to describe himself as an atheist. Despite his disbelief in the resurrection, Ehrman admits:

> I am struck by a certain consistency among otherwise independent witnesses in placing Mary Magdalene both at the cross and at the tomb on the third day. . . . It seems hard to believe that this just happened by way of a fluke of storytelling. It seems much more likely that, at least with the traditions involving the empty tomb, we are dealing with something actually rooted in history.[41]

New Testament scholar Paula Fredriksen is not a Christian. Yet, as she reads the reports of the earliest followers of Jesus, she is open-minded enough to recognize that

in their own terms what they saw was the raised Jesus.
. . . All the historic evidence we have afterwards attests
to their conviction that that's what they saw. I'm not
saying that they really did see the raised Jesus. . . . I don't
know what they saw. But I do know, as a historian, that
they must have seen something.[42]

Even people who aren't Christians can essentially admit,
"We are dealing with something actually rooted in history,"
and "the earliest witnesses must have seen something." But
what was it that the first followers of Jesus saw?

Christians have always believed these first witnesses
saw Jesus himself in risen flesh. Yet the question we are
exploring together is whether or not the resurrection really
happened, and anyone who is interested in that question
is likely to wonder about possibilities that do not involve
a corpse coming back to life.

So what are the alternatives to bodily resurrection? And
how probable are these possibilities?

Taylor Swift's Grandmother and the Empty Tomb
One of the most prominent possibilities is that the first
witnesses sensed a postmortem presence they misinter-
preted as resurrection.

In the weeks and months after a loved one dies, it is not uncommon for friends or family members to sense the nearby presence of the deceased person. In the words of Taylor Swift, reflecting on her feeling that her deceased grandmother Marjorie was still present and conversing with her,

If I didn't know better,
I'd think you were still around.[43]

Sometimes, this sense that a loved one is "still around" can take the form of visions that seem physical. It is even possible for groups of people to experience collective hallucinations.[44]

Might that have happened among the first followers of Jesus?

What if the alleged witnesses merely experienced a profound sense of their crucified leader's presence that they misperceived as resurrection? Or suppose a few of them hallucinated or experienced a vision that convinced them they saw Jesus alive in the flesh. If so, what the disciples witnessed was not a body transformed and restored to life. At best, what happened was more like the experience of the boy in *The Sixth Sense* who interacted with dead people who did not know they were dead. At worst, they were duped by a collective hallucination. Either way, Jesus is no more alive today than Taylor Swift's grandmother.

But there is a problem with this proposition.

Neither visions nor hallucinations can cause a tomb to be empty.

Or, to put it another way, even if Grandma Marjorie's spirit accompanied Taylor on her latest tour, Marjorie's remains would remain in the ground. The body of Jesus, however, is nowhere to be found.

That is why the traditions involving the empty tomb are so important. One key claim that is consistent throughout multiple retellings of the story is that Mary Magdalene saw the cave where the corpse of Jesus was laid and returned to find the tomb empty on the third day (Matt. 27:61–28:7; Mark 15:47–16:7; Luke 23:55–24:11).[45] It is difficult to make any reasonable case that the body of Jesus was still buried when Mary visited the tomb. If his body were still entombed behind the rolling stone when people began to proclaim he was alive, the religious leaders could have quickly confounded every claim of resurrection by disinterring the dead body and parading the corpse through the streets of Jerusalem. Such an act would have ended the earliest disciples' devotion to the risen Jesus while their claims were still confined to a tiny sect. But the religious leaders apparently never attempted anything of this sort, which suggests the body was no longer accessible to them.

If the tomb was truly empty—and it certainly seems to have been—it becomes very difficult to dismiss the disciples' experiences as visions or hallucinations. But it is not merely the emptiness of the tomb that makes me confident Jesus was raised from the dead. It is also the deaths of the witnesses.

What People Won't Die for—and What They Will

"I only believe histories in which witnesses were to be slaughtered," French philosopher Blaise Pascal once wrote.[46] It's a bit of an overstatement, but there's also a kernel of common sense in Pascal's words. Historical claims are most believable when witnesses refuse to alter their claims even in the face of death.

Of course, martyrdom by itself doesn't prove the martyr's account of an alleged event. Myriads of people throughout history have died for lies they thought were true. What makes a claim most believable is when the martyrs are in a position to know firsthand whether or not their testimony is true. If you're uncertain about a claim you're making, or if you know the claim is false, you will back away from the story at some point before it costs you your life.

Atheists around the world have declared themselves members of the satirical Church of the Flying Spaghetti Monster (yes, it's an actual organization that claims "millions, if not thousands" of followers).[47] And yet, not one of these individuals will ever die for this cause, because they know their "Pastafarian" faith is a hoax. The principle that prevents Pastafarian martyrs is not limited to hoax religions. Throughout history, people have sometimes sacrificed their lives for lies, but human beings are not typically willing to die for what they know is a falsehood.

Which brings us to a crucial question about the resurrection: Did any of those who claimed to have seen the risen Jesus persist in their devotion to this message at the cost of their lives?

The answer is yes—and not merely one, but at least three.

*How the Martyrdoms of Eyewitnesses
Make the Resurrection Credible*

Multiple early sources testify together that no fewer than three alleged witnesses of the resurrection died for what they declared: Simon Peter, James the brother of Jesus, and James the son of Zebedee.[48]

- James the son of Zebedee was beheaded in the AD 40s by King Herod Agrippa I to please the religious leaders in Jerusalem, according to reports from Luke (Acts 12:1–3) and Clement of Alexandria.[49]
- The high priest Ananus had James the brother of Jesus stoned to death around AD 61, according to Josephus and Eusebius.[50]
- Peter was executed in Rome—perhaps by crucifixion—during the reign of Emperor Nero in the AD 60s. John's Gospel (21:18–19) as well as a letter written by Clement of Rome hint at Peter's martyrdom, and other writers explicitly mention how he died for his faith.[51]

If the claims of resurrection had been falsified, one or more of these leaders would almost certainly have been in a position to know about the fabrication. If the disciples stole the body of Jesus, as some Jewish religious leaders claimed (Matt. 28:11–15), or if their encounters with his resurrected flesh were ambiguous, these three would have been aware of that, too.

Once their claims about Jesus caused them to be ostracized by fellow Jews, Peter and the two Jameses had nothing to gain by continuing to proclaim the resurrection. Especially after their claims about Jesus exposed them to localized outbursts of Roman persecution, they knew they had everything to lose by continuing to insist Jesus was alive. Still, they chose death over any denial of their devotion to the risen Jesus. They persisted to the point of execution, and their persistence provides strong evidence for the resurrection's reality.

When I was a college student struggling with my faith, this aspect of the evidence seized me at a moment when I thought the last dregs of faith had been drained from my soul. People sometimes die for lies, but they do not typically die for a lie they know to be a lie. Yet witnesses who would have known if the resurrection had been a fabrication clung to their confidence that Jesus was alive all the way to their deaths. That recognition shook my skepticism and forced me to doubt my doubts. Decades later, it still does. When

I consider these evidences, I find myself convinced that the resurrection is only implausible if we presuppose a world where miracles are historically impossible.

But that's not all.

There is at least one more historical reason to believe Jesus really rose from the dead. This one has to do with the sheer unlikelihood that a movement that started with a crucified Jewish teacher could multiply in the ways it did unless the first witnesses experienced something supernatural. To take a look at this evidence, follow me to the Palatine Hill in the city of Rome.

The Vulgarity of the Cross and the Reality of the Resurrection

A few blocks from the Colosseum and the Arch of Constantine, a piece of plaster is mounted on a wall in the Museo Palatino. The plaster appears blank at first glance, and you might wonder why the fragment has been so carefully affixed to the wall. But then you look closer, and you notice a bit of crude graffiti gouged into the surface. This obscene etching from the late second or early third century AD depicts a man with the head of a donkey hanging from a cross, with his posterior exposed. At the foot of the cross, a man wearing the sleeveless tunic of a slave prays with an outstretched hand. Three words have been scratched around the praying figure; the misspelled Greek clause can be translated into English as "Alexamenos worships God" (see fig. 1).

Figure 1. *Alexamenos Graffito* (Wikimedia Commons). Discovered in a dormitory where imperial pages were trained, this graffito seems to depict Jesus on a cross with the head of a donkey.

The aim of the unknown graffiti artist seems to have been to mock an enslaved person named Alexamenos, who had devoted himself to Jesus.[52] This artifact stands as a silent reminder of how shocking the reports about Jesus seemed to ancient Romans. Followers of this new way had devoted their lives to a deity who endured a death reserved for traitors and slaves. The very word *crucify* was a vulgarity in ancient Rome, spoken sparingly in polite company.[53] The Jewish historian Josephus referred to crucifixion as "that most wretched of deaths."[54] Nevertheless, Christians persisted in praising a crucified God. Even more embarrassing from the perspective of their neighbors, the Christian deity apparently did not leave his body behind and ascend to the realm of the gods after he died, which is what any self-respecting deity would surely do. Instead, according to the Christians, the same scarred body that died was raised to life and transformed into the first sign of God's new creation.

Despite making such distasteful claims, the movement multiplied. By the end of the first century, the news that a crucified Jew had returned to life had spanned the Roman Empire from Syria to Spain, and four written retellings of his life were circulating in the empire's largest cities. Despite sporadic local persecutions, the communities that devoted themselves to Jesus kept gaining adherents. After failing in their attempts to crush Christian communities through a series of empire-wide persecutions in the late third and early fourth centuries, the emperors finally gave up their efforts to force Christians to sacrifice to the venerable gods of Rome.

Looking back on this remarkable sequence of events, Augustine of Hippo saw evidence that the resurrection had really happened. He wrote:

> Now, we have three incredible things, and yet all three have come to pass: First, it is incredible that Christ rose in the flesh and ascended with his flesh into heaven. Second, it is incredible that the world has come to believe something so incredible. Third, it is incredible that a few unknown men, with no standing and no education, were able to persuade the world . . . of something so incredible.
>
> Of these three incredible things, the people we are debating refuse to believe the first, they are compelled to grant the second, but they cannot explain how the

second happened unless they believe the third. . . .
And, if they still refuse to believe that Christ's apostles
really did work miracles to convince people to believe
in the message of Christ's resurrection and ascension,
they leave us with one even greater miracle: that the
whole world has somehow come to believe in a miracle
without any miracles at all.[55]

For Augustine, the spread of the church in the aftermath
of the crucifixion provided evidence for the truth of the
resurrection. Unless the first witnesses actually saw death
reversed, it seems almost impossible that they would have
persisted in their proclamation about a crucified man. "The
founders of the other great world religions died peacefully,
surrounded by their followers and the knowledge that their
movement was growing," Tim Keller once pointed out. "In
contrast, Jesus died in disgrace, betrayed, denied, and abandoned by everyone."[56] Unlike Confucius and Siddhartha
Gautama, who spent many years training their disciples,
Jesus taught his disciples for only three years or so. Unlike
Muhammad, Jesus died in humiliation, with no armies,
no wealth, and no heirs.[57] Yet the message of his death and
resurrection eventually conquered an empire.

What about You?

At the end of their quest to save the Shire, Frodo said to Sam on the slopes of Mount Doom, "I am glad you are here with me. Here at the end of all things."[58] And I am glad *you* are still here with me, here at the end of this book.

My hope is that at the very least, you have recognized that faith in the resurrection can be grounded in evidence. Most of the evidence I have presented has been historical, but there is one piece of evidence that is not so much historical as personal. Whether or not you think the resurrection of Jesus happened, there is a longing for resurrection inside you. You yearn for a world where all things are made right and new. You long for a realm where death no longer reigns. You may not want Jesus, but you want resurrection.

Perhaps these yearnings are merely empty fantasies and wishful thinking. But what if they aren't? What if you were made with a longing for life that never ends? If so, maybe your aching for eternity is not a defect in your mind but a part of your design.

If you still disbelieve the resurrection, or if you are not sure what to think about a man returning from the dead, my encouragement to you is to read the four New Testament Gospels with an open mind. Consider the claims of Jesus, and hear this invitation Augustine spoke to his fifth-century congregation in North Africa:

> Jesus . . . promised us his life, but what he actually did is even more unbelievable; he paid us his death in advance. [It is as if Jesus said,] "I'm inviting you to my life, where nobody dies, where life is truly happy, . . . to the region of the angels, to the friendship of the Father and the Holy Spirit, to the everlasting supper, to be my brothers and sisters. . . . I'm inviting you to my life."[59]

By suffering the punishment for sin in our place, the crucified Christ made a way for you and me to have fellowship with him through faith. Through his resurrection, the same Christ opened the door for us to share in his eternal life. Will you at least consider the possibility that all of this might be true?

If you already believe the resurrection, I hope this book has multiplied your confidence that, in the words of U2,

> the stone it has been moved,
> the grave is now a groove.[60]

But I want more for you than an increase in your faith. If Jesus has truly been raised from the dead, every victory has been won. The kingdom that is yet to come has burst into our present world, and that present-yet-future kingdom is your true home. The resurrection of Jesus guarantees the renovation of the world. That's why

> we are not those without hope, or hoping in hope alone.
> Resurrection shows that this land is not our home.[61]

Because every wrong will be made right, you can forgive, trusting that God will deal with every sin and abuse of his creation in his time and in his way. Since Jesus has been revealed as the risen King of all creation, you can be set free from placing your hope in earthly political allegiances. Because your future home is guaranteed to be a place of perfect peace and justice, you can commit yourself to practicing peace and justice in the present. In the words of Esau McCaulley,

> If the resurrection is true, and the Christian stakes his or her entire existence on its truthfulness, then

our peaceful witness testifies to a new and better way of being human that transcends the endless cycle of violence.[62]

If Jesus left behind an empty tomb—and there is good evidence that he did—that changes everything.

What will the resurrection change for you?

Notes

1. For wild dogs and scavenging birds in the aftermath of crucifixion, see, e.g., Apuleius, *Metamorphoses: Books 1–6*, ed. and trans. J. Arthur Hanson (Cambridge, MA: Harvard University Press, 1996), 6.32.1; Juvenal, "The Satires of Juvenal," in *Juvenal and Persius*, ed. and trans. Susanna Morton Braund (Cambridge, MA: Harvard University Press, 2004), 14.77–78.

2. My translation. See Josephus, *The Jewish War: Books 5–7*, trans. H. St. J. Thackeray (Cambridge, MA: Harvard University Press, 1971), 5.449–51; see also Seneca, "*De Consolatione ad Marciam*," in *Moral Essays*, trans. John W. Basore, vol. 2 (Cambridge, MA: Harvard University Press, 1932), 20.3.

3. Augustine, *Expositions of the Psalms*, vol. 5, *99–120*, trans. Maria Boulding (Hyde Park, NY: New City, 2004), 120:6.

4. James George Frazier, *Adonis, Attis, Osiris: Studies in the History of Oriental Religion*, vol. 5 of *The Golden Bough*, 3rd ed. (Cambridge, UK: Cambridge University Press, 1914), 3–12, 298–312.

5. Bertrand Russell, *Why I Am Not a Christian* (London: Allen and Unwin, 1957), 12.

6. See, e.g., John Dominic Crossan, *Jesus: A Revolutionary Biography* (1994; repr., New York: HarperOne, 2009), 144–50; Bart D. Ehrman, *Did Jesus Exist? The Historical Argument for Jesus of Nazareth* (New York: HarperOne, 2013), 332–40; Gerd Lüdemann, *The Resurrection of Christ: A Historical Inquiry* (Amherst, NY: Prometheus, 2004), 50; Robert J. Miller, *The Jesus Seminar and Its Critics* (Santa Rosa, CA: Polebridge, 1999), 38.

7. C. S. Lewis, *God in the Dock* (Grand Rapids, MI: Eerdmans, 1970), 58–60; see also Lewis, *Surprised by Joy* (New York: Harcourt Brace, 1955), 228, 274.

8. Richard Dawkins, *The Selfish Gene* (Oxford, UK: Oxford University Press, 1989), 330; Dawkins, quoted in "Did Jesus Really Rise from the Dead?," *The Spectator*, April 15, 2006, http://www.spectator.co.uk.

9. Augustine of Hippo, *On Faith in Things Unseen*, trans. Joseph Deferrari and Mary Francis McDonald, in *The*

Immortality of the Soul; The Magnitude of the Soul; On Music; The Advantage of Believing; On Faith in Things Unseen (1947; repr., Washington, DC: Catholic University of America Press, 2002), 3.

10. Timothy Keller, *Hope in Times of Fear: The Resurrection and the Meaning of Easter* (New York: Viking, 2021), 15.

11. Bart Ehrman, quoted in Gary Kamiya, "Jesus Is Just Alright with Him," *Salon*, April 3, 2009, http://www.salon.com.

12. Rhett McLaughlin, "Rhett's Spiritual Deconstruction—3 Years Later," *Ear Biscuits with Rhett & Link*, no. 369, February 12, 2023, http://www.searchicality.com.

13. G. K. Chesterton, *The Everlasting Man* (1925; repr., Moscow, ID: Canon, 2021), 271.

14. J. W. S. Arnold, "The Kentucky Meat Shower," *American Journal of Microscopy and Popular Science* 1, no. 7 (June 1876): 84; "The Carnal Rain," *New York Herald*, March 21, 1876; "Flesh Descending in a Shower," *New York Times*, March 10, 1876; L. D. Kastenbine, "The Kentucky Meat Shower," *Louisville Medical News* 1, no. 21 (May 20, 1876): 254–55. See also Colin Dickey, *The Unidentified: Mythical Monsters, Alien Encounters, and*

Our Obsession with the Unexplained (New York: Viking, 2020), 41–44, 280–81.

15. The story of the Kentucky meat shower is also recounted in Timothy Paul Jones, "Meat from the Sky and the Resurrection's Plausibility," The Gospel Coalition, April 14, 2022, https://www.thegospelcoalition.org, and Jones, *Why Should I Trust the Bible?* (Fearn, UK: Christian Focus, 2020), 63–64.

16. Origen of Alexandria, *Contra Celsum: Libri VIII*, ed. Miroslav Marcovich (Boston: Brill, 2001), 3.26–27.

17. Tom Harpur, *The Pagan Christ: Recovering the Lost Light* (New York: Walker, 2004), 84.

18. Lewis, *God in the Dock*, 58–60.

19. Emily Teeter, *Religion and Ritual in Ancient Egypt* (Cambridge, UK: Cambridge University Press, 2011), 175.

20. J. R. R. Tolkien, *The Two Towers*, pt. 2 of *The Lord of the Rings*, 1 vol. ed. (New York: Houghton Mifflin, 1994), 484, 490–91.

21. Tryggve N. D. Mettinger, *The Riddle of Resurrection: "Dying and Rising Gods" in the Ancient Near East* (University Park, PA: Eisenbrauns, 2013), 221.

22. Euripides, "Alcestis," in *Cyclops. Alcestis. Medea*, ed. and trans. David Kovacs (Cambridge, MA: Harvard

University Press, 1994), 1123–58. The poet Aristeas was thought by some to have reappeared after mysteriously vanishing, yet some of his reappearances were separated by centuries, and his later reappearances were never clearly physical. See Herodotus, *The Persian Wars: Books 3–4*, trans. A. D. Godley (Cambridge, MA: Harvard University Press, 1921), 4.13–15.

23. Origen, *Contra Celsum* 2.55.

24. Plato, "Timaeus," in *Timaeus. Critias. Cleitophon. Menexenus. Epistles* (Cambridge, MA: Harvard University Press, 1929), 41d–e. See also Cicero, *"De Re Publica,"* in *On the Republic. On the Laws*, trans. Clinton W. Keyes (Cambridge, MA: Harvard University Press, 1928), 6.15–16.

25. N. T. Wright, *The Resurrection of the Son of God* (Minneapolis: Fortress, 2003), 60.

26. Wright, *Resurrection*, 131–42.

27. The raising of saints in association with the death and resurrection of Jesus does not contradict this expectation (Matt. 27:53); the historical resurrection of particular saints pointed proleptically to future resurrection but still remained something less than a resurrection of all the righteous. See Craig S. Keener, *The Gospel of*

Matthew: A Socio-Rhetorical Commentary (Grand Rapids, MI: Eerdmans, 2009), 686.

28. See Josephus, *The Jewish War* 7.2.1–7.5.7; Josephus, *Jewish Antiquities: Book 20*, trans. Louis H. Feldman (Cambridge, MA: Harvard University Press, 1965), 20.5.1; Craig A. Evans, *Jesus and His Contemporaries: Comparative Studies* (Boston: Brill, 2001), 183–211.

29. Gordon D. Fee, *The First Epistle to the Corinthians*, rev. ed. (Grand Rapids, MI: Eerdmans, 2014), 5–7, 20–23, 802.

30. Simon Gathercole, *The Gospel and the Gospels: Christian Proclamation and Early Jesus Books* (Grand Rapids, MI: Eerdmans, 2022), 44, 117. Vanishing into the realm of the gods was not unknown in Roman narratives. See, e.g., Livy, *History of Rome: Books 1–2*, trans. B. O. Foster (Cambridge, MA: Harvard University Press, 1919), 1.16; Diodorus Siculus, *Library of History: Books 2.35–4.58*, trans. C. H. Oldfather (Cambridge, MA: Harvard University Press, 1935), 4.38.

31. Larry W. Hurtado, *Lord Jesus Christ: Devotion to Jesus in Earliest Christianity* (Grand Rapids, MI: Eerdmans, 2005), 168–76, 215–16.

32. Hurtado, *Lord Jesus Christ*, 83.

33. Some portions are adapted from Jones, *Why Should I Trust the Bible?*, 68–69. For further references, see Richard Bauckham, *Jesus and the Eyewitnesses: The Gospels as Eyewitness Testimony*, 2nd ed. (Grand Rapids, MI: Eerdmans, 2017), 39–92, and Peter J. Williams, *Can We Trust the Gospels?* (Wheaton, IL: Crossway, 2018), 51–86.

34. On the authorship of the Gospels, see Eusebius, *Ecclesiastical History: Books 1–5*, trans. Kirsopp Lake (Cambridge, MA: Harvard University Press, 1926), 5.8.2–4; Irenaeus of Lyon, *Libros Quinque Adversus Haereses*, vol. 2, ed. W. W. Harvey (1857; repr., Rochester, NY: St. Irenaeus, 2013), 3.1.1–2; Tertullian, *Adversus Marcionem: Books 4–5*, ed. and trans. Ernest Evans (Oxford, UK: Clarendon, 1972), 4.2. See also Charles E. Hill, "What Papias Said about John (and Luke)," *Journal of Theological Studies* 49 (1998): 582–629.

35. Lewis, *God in the Dock*, 58–60. See also Lewis, *Surprised by Joy*, 228, 274.

36. Bec Crew, "The Great Kentucky Meat Shower Mystery Unwound by Projectile Vulture Vomit," *Scientific American*, December 1, 2014, http://www.scientificamerican.com.

37. Richard Dawkins, "You Ask the Questions Special," *Independent*, December 4, 2006, http://www.independent.co.uk.

38. See Gospel of Peter 9 (34), 12–13 (50–57), in P. Cair. 10759, folios 3v, 4v, 5r, and 5v, translated in Paul Foster, *The Gospel of Peter* (Boston: Brill, 2010), 201–5.

39. Tacitus, *Annals: Books 13–16*, trans. John Jackson (Cambridge, MA: Harvard University Press, 1937), 15.44.

40. Josephus, *Jewish Antiquities: Books 4–6*, trans. H. St. J. Thackeray and Ralph Marcus (Cambridge, MA: Harvard University Press, 1930), 4.219. See also Origen, *Contra Celsum* 2.55.

41. Bart D. Ehrman, *Peter, Paul, and Mary Magdalene: The Followers of Jesus in History and Legend* (New York: Oxford University Press, 2006), 226.

42. Paula Fredriksen, interview by Peter Jennings, *The Search for Jesus*, ABC, June 26, 2000.

43. Taylor Swift, "Marjorie," by Aaron Dessner and Taylor Swift, track 13 on *Evermore*, Sony/ATV Music Publishing and Universal Publishing Group, 2020.

44. Dale C. Allison Jr., *Resurrection of Jesus: Apologetics, Polemics, History* (New York: Bloomsbury, 2021), 215–16, 228–29, 233–34, 241–46, 249–51.

45. See also Gospel of Peter 6–9 (24–34), 12–13 (50–55).

46. Blaise Pascal, *Pensées*, trans. Roger Ariew (Indianapolis: Hackett, 2004), 204 (S663/L822).

47. Peter Timms, "Pasta Strainers and Pirates: How the Church of the Flying Spaghetti Monster Was Born," *The Guardian*, May 17, 2019, http://www.theguardian.com.

48. Sean McDowell, "A Historical Evaluation of the Evidence for the Deaths of the Apostles as Martyrs for Their Faith" (PhD diss., The Southern Baptist Theological Seminary, 2014), 103–54, 194–258, 424–29; McDowell, *The Fate of the Apostles: Examining the Martyrdom Accounts of the Closest Followers of Jesus* (New York: Routledge, 2015), 55–92, 115–56.

49. Eusebius, *Ecclesiastical History* 2.9.1–3.

50. Josephus, *Jewish Antiquities* 20.9.1–2; Eusebius, *Ecclesiastical History* 2.1.4–5. Additionally, James the brother of Jesus may have been pushed from the steps or the parapet of the temple. See also Richard Bauckham, "For What Offence Was James Put to Death?," in *James the Just and Christian Origins*, ed. Bruce Chilton and Craig Evans (Boston: Brill, 1999), 205–26.

51. Clement, "First Letter to the Corinthians," in *The Apostolic Fathers*, vol. 1, *I Clement. II Clement. Ignatius. Polycarp. Didache*, ed. and trans. Bart D. Ehrman (Cambridge, MA: Harvard University Press, 2003), 5.1–5; Eusebius, *Ecclesiastical History* 3.1.2. See also

Richard Bauckham, "The Martyrdom of Peter in Early Christian Literature," in *Rise and Decline of the Roman World*, ed. Wolfgang Haase and Hildegard Temporini, vol. 26 (New York: Walter de Gruyter, 1992), 17, 550–88; Oscar Cullmann, *Peter: Disciple, Apostle, Martyr* (Waco, TX: Baylor University Press, 2011).

52. Peter Keegan, "Reading the 'Pages' of the Domus Caesaris," in *Roman Slavery and Roman Material Culture*, ed. Michele George (Cambridge, UK: Cambridge University Press, 2012), 69–98; James Tschen-Emmons, *Artifacts from Ancient Rome* (Santa Barbara, CA: Greenwood, 2014), 15–18. For a literary example of mockery of the cross, see Lucian, "The Consonants at Law," in *Phalaris. Hippias or The Bath. Dionysus. Heracles. Amber or The Swans. The Fly. Nigrinus. Demonax. The Hall. My Native Land. Octogenarians. A True Story. Slander. The Consonants at Law. The Carousal*, trans. A. M. Harmon (Cambridge, MA: Harvard University Press, 1913), 12.

53. Martin Hengel, *Crucifixion in the Ancient World and the Folly of the Message of the Cross* (Philadelphia: Fortress, 1977), 10–11.

54. Josephus, *The Jewish War* 7.203.

55. My translation. See Augustine of Hippo, *City of God: Books 21–22*, trans. William M. Green (Cambridge, MA: Harvard University Press, 1972), 22.5.

56. Keller, *Hope in Times of Fear*, 80.

57. Hans Küng, *On Being a Christian* (New York: Doubleday, 1984), 335–46.

58. J. R. R. Tolkien, *The Return of the King*, pt. 3 of *The Lord of the Rings*, 926.

59. Augustine of Hippo, *Sermons (230–72B) on the Liturgical Seasons*, trans. Edmund Hill (Hyde Park, NY: New City, 1993), 231.5. See also Augustine of Hippo, *The Trinity*, trans. John Rotelle (Hyde Park, NY: New City, 1991), 13.3.8.

60. U2, "Window in the Skies," track 18 on *U218 Singles*, Mercury/Interscope, 2006.

61. Propaganda, "Made Straight," track 13 on *Crooked*, Humble Beast, 2016.

62. Esau McCaulley, *Reading While Black: African American Biblical Interpretation as an Exercise in Hope* (Downers Grove, IL: InterVarsity, 2020), 34.

Recommended Resources

Bauckham, Richard. *Jesus and the Eyewitnesses: The Gospels as Eyewitness Testimony*. Grand Rapids, MI: Eerdmans, 2017. This scholarly work focuses on the question of whether or not the New Testament Gospels were based on eyewitness testimony. Bauckham convincingly demonstrates the eyewitness origins of the Gospel stories.

Chase, Mitchell L. *Resurrection Hope and the Death of Death.* Wheaton, IL: Crossway, 2022. In this brief biblical theology of the resurrection, the author shows how hope for bodily resurrection is present throughout Scripture, while recognizing that Jews in the first century weren't anticipating the death and resurrection of the Messiah.

Licona, Michael. *The Resurrection of Jesus: A New Historiographical Approach*. Downers Grove, IL: IVP Academic, 2010. Licona examines every alternative and provides a thorough and sober scholarly analysis of the historical probability of Jesus's resurrection.

McDowell, Sean. *The Fate of the Apostles: Examining the Martyrdom Accounts of the Closest Followers of Jesus.* New York: Routledge, 2018. Well-intended apologists have frequently overstated the evidence for the martyrdoms of the apostles. This balanced, scholarly work carefully analyzes the historical sources.

McLaughlin, Rebecca. *Is Easter Unbelievable? Four Questions Everyone Should Ask about the Resurrection Story.* Charlotte, NC: Good Book, 2023. In this brief and breezy survey, McLaughlin shows that the life of Jesus was historical, the death of Jesus ethical, and the resurrection of Jesus credible.

Wallace, J. Warner. *Cold-Case Christianity: A Homicide Detective Investigates the Claims of the Gospels.* Colorado Springs: Cook, 2013. Wallace is a cold-case detective and a former atheist. In this short book, he applies his detective skills to the question of whether or not Jesus really rose from the dead.

Williams, Peter J. *Can We Trust the Gospels?* Wheaton, IL: Crossway, 2018. A surprisingly concise book considering how much content it covers, *Can We Trust the Gospels?*

builds a solid case for the reliability of the Gospels. If you have doubts about the truthfulness of these biblical books, Williams's volume is the place to begin.

Wright, N. T. *The Resurrection of the Son of God*. Minneapolis: Fortress, 2003. After critiquing modern biases that rule out miraculous events in history, this scholarly work maps out Jewish and Greco-Roman beliefs about life after death. Resurrection is shown to be the most likely explanation for the empty tomb and the early reports of the risen Jesus.

Scripture Index

TGC THE GOSPEL COALITION

The Gospel Coalition (TGC) supports the church in making disciples of all nations, by providing gospel-centered resources that are trusted and timely, winsome and wise.

Guided by a Council of more than 40 pastors in the Reformed tradition, TGC seeks to advance gospel-centered ministry for the next generation by producing content (including articles, podcasts, videos, courses, and books) and convening leaders (including conferences, virtual events, training, and regional chapters).

In all of this we want to help Christians around the world better grasp the gospel of Jesus Christ and apply it to all of life in the 21st century. We want to offer biblical truth in an era of great confusion. We want to offer gospel-centered hope for the searching.

Join us by visiting TGC.org so you can be equipped to love God with all your heart, soul, mind, and strength, and to love your neighbor as yourself.

TGC.org

TGC HARD QUESTIONS

Does God Care about Gender Identity?

Samuel D. Ferguson

Is Christianity Good for the World?

Sharon James

What Does Depression Mean for My Faith?

Kathryn Butler, MD

Why Do We Feel Lonely at Church?

Jeremy Linneman

Where Is God in a World with So Much Evil?

Colin Hansen

Did the Resurrection Really Happen?

Timothy Paul Jones

The series TGC Hard Questions serves the church by providing tools that answer people's deep *longings* for community, their *concerns* about biblical ethics, and their *doubts* about confessional faith.

For more information, visit **crossway.org**.